THE FBI STORY

The FBI and ORGANIZED CRIME

By Dale Anderson

MASON CREST PUBLISHERS

Produced in association with Water Buffalo Books.
Design by Westgraphix LLC.

MASON CREST PUBLISHERS INC.
370 Reed Road
Broomall, Pennsylvania 19008
(866) MCP-BOOK (toll free)
www.masoncrest.com

Printed in the United States of America

First Printing

9 8 7 6 5 4 3 2 1

Library of Congress Cataloging-in-Publication Data

Anderson, Dale, 1953-
        The FBI and organized crime / Dale Anderson.
            p. cm. — (The FBI story)
        Includes bibliographical references and index.
        ISBN 978-1-4222-0565-5 (hardcover) — ISBN 978-1-4222-1372-8 (pbk.)
    1. United States. Federal Bureau of Investigation—Juvenile literature.
    2. Organized crime—United States—History—Juvenile literature. I. Title.
    HV6769.A63 2009
    363.250973—dc22   2008047902

Photo credits: © AP/Wide World Photos: 6, 13b, 13e, 13f, 16, 20, 22, 25a, 26, 27,
29a, 30, 34 (both), 37, 38, 39, 42, 47, 49, 54, 55; © CORBIS: 8, 11, 24, 51;
© Courtesy of FBI: cover (upper left, center left, lower left, lower right), 1, 7, 14, 15b, 25a,
29b, 31, 33, 43, 46, 50, 52, 53, 57 (both), 60 (both); © Getty Images: 4, 13a, 13c, 15a, 40;
Courtesy of the Prints and Photographs Division, Library of Congress: cover (center), 13d.

Publisher's note:
All quotations in this book come from original sources and contain the spelling and grammatical
inconsistencies of the original text.

CONTENTS

1 The Undercover Man

It was a routine meeting among criminals, but one that could turn deadly dangerous at any moment. New York mobsters had some stolen watches and were talking to a group of **fences** about selling them. As the fences came into the room, a member of the New York group eyed one of the fences warily. This man, the mobster knew, could mean the death of him.

Playing It Cool

Why was the fence such a threat? The worried mobster was actually agent Joe Pistone. He was working **undercover** for the Federal Bureau of Investigation (FBI), pretending to be

In 1976, FBI agent Joe Pistone went undercover, took the name Donnie Brasco, and infiltrated the mob. He is shown here in 1997 as an adviser to the motion picture *Donnie Brasco*, based on Pistone's autobiographical book of the

a criminal named Donnie Brasco. Pistone's job was to gather as much information as he could about New York's organized crime families and the crimes they committed. The fence was a threat because Pistone had arrested him two years earlier. If the fence recognized him—and said that Pistone had been in the FBI—the mobsters would shoot Pistone on the spot.

Pistone played it cool. He did not leave the room. He wanted to keep the fence in his sights at all times so he could gauge his reactions. After a while, he had a conversation with the fence about his ability to handle certain kinds of stolen goods. The fence showed no signs of recognizing him. Pistone could breathe easily again.

The meeting with the fence was just one of the many moments that Joe Pistone's life was on the line over a period of nearly six years. During that time, he managed to gain acceptance in one of New York City's **Mafia** crime families. He lived like mobsters, talked like them, and acted like them. He learned who committed what crimes, and when, and how. And Pistone carefully reported everything back to the FBI. All the time, he knew that the slightest slipup would make him a dead man.

Background

Joe Pistone had joined the FBI in 1969. Working in the Tampa, Florida, field office, he did an undercover investigation.

It was successful, resulting in the arrest of more than 30 criminals. Pistone was congratulated for his excellent work and transferred to the New York field office. Soon he and his superiors decided to send him underground again.

In September of 1976, Pistone started his new life as criminal Don Brasco. He pretended to be a burglar and a jewel thief, taking time to learn about gems before he went underground. He also pretended to be an orphan, so there would be no family members that gangsters could call to get information about him.

Getting Accepted

Pistone gradually got to know members of the Bonanno crime family. Slowly, he got them to gain confidence that he was a criminal and could be trusted. In *Donnie Brasco*, the

Joseph Bonanno, Jr. (left), and Salvatore "Bill" Bonanno, sons of mobster "Joe Bananas" Bonanno, are shown as they appeared for questioning before a grand jury in 1965. As one of the original five Mafia families in New York, the Bonannos were involved in a wide range of illegal activities, including gambling, **extortion**, drugs, and prostitution. As "Donnie Brasco," Joe Pistone had worked his way into the family by gaining the confidence of its most important members. He had to give up his undercover role, however, when he was ordered to carry out a hit on a rival mobster.

book he wrote about his undercover work, he explained why he moved slowly:

> You push a little here and there, but very gently. . . . Above all, you cannot hurry. You cannot seem eager to meet certain people, make certain contacts, learn about certain scores [crimes]. The quickest way to get tagged as a cop is to try to move too fast.

Pistone—or Brasco—had to be careful. He made sure that he was never followed when he went to meet an FBI agent—or to see his wife. He never took notes about what he saw or heard. He worried that someone, either a mobster or the police, might search him or his apartment. If they found those notes, his undercover

FINDING AN AGENT

Working undercover is very complicated. The law enforcement officer has to be a convincing criminal. He or she also has to be willing to live with the danger that Joseph Pistone lived through, knowing that one's life is always on the line.

Undercover officers also have to fit in with the lifestyle and activities of the criminal group being targeted. Joe Pistone fell into his first undercover job almost by accident. His second job—invading the New York City mob—was a natural outgrowth of the first. Still, finding the right agent for undercover work can be difficult. The FBI makes that task easier now by keeping a database of the hobbies, backgrounds, and interests of agents interested in undercover work. The Bureau can then pick the agent who fits with the needed job. When the FBI decided to go after a Texas motorcycle gang known for selling drugs, officials found Dennis Dufour in the database. He had ridden motorcycles as a teen and had experience investigating drug dealers.

life would be gone. Instead, he would call an FBI agent every few days and relate new information he had. Later, Pistone wore microphones and a tape recorder.

With those, he recorded conversations that could be used against the mobsters. Eventually, one gang member, Benjamin

Johnny Depp (left) starred as Joe Pistone in the 1997 movie *Donnie Brasco*. Al Pacino (right) portrayed Lefty Ruggiero, the mobster who took in "Donnie Brasco" as his partner.

"Lefty Guns" Ruggiero, made Pistone his partner. Though not an official member of the Mafia, Pistone was as close as he could get.

Over the years, Ruggiero taught Pistone the ways of the mob world. He also told many stories to Pistone, who passed the information along to his contacts in the Bureau. Eventually, Pistone traveled to Miami, Los Angeles, and Milwaukee and made contact with mob figures there. Since he was connected in New York, he was accepted in these other cities, too. That allowed him to win acceptance for other undercover agents in those cities. He passed those agents off to the mob as trustworthy, too.

Putting an End to It

After six years, Pistone finally had to end his undercover work. A fight for control had broken out within the Bonanno family. One of the mobsters ordered Pistone to kill someone. If he did, he would rise higher in the confidence of the family members and be able to learn even more secrets. But the FBI would not condone his carrying out a killing. Louis Freeh, who in 1993 would become director of the FBI, but in the early 1980s was a **prosecutor** working in New York, later explained the problem in a memoir: "Penetrating the mob was one thing, but doing its dirty work, actually whacking somebody, was way beyond the bounds of the possible."

Prosecutors had to scramble to pull together all the evidence Pistone had provided. They got **indictments** against nearly two dozen people, and FBI agents moved in to make arrests. Pistone was hidden away for his safety.

The FBI also picked up Lefty Ruggiero. Agents knew that because he was connected to Pistone, the Bonanno family would kill him. That is precisely what happened to two other mobsters who had worked with Pistone. One was assassinated soon after Pistone disappeared. The other was killed the following year. But Ruggiero refused to testify against his mob bosses, even though they wanted to kill him. He was convicted and sentenced to prison.

Coming to Trial

Even after Pistone ended his undercover work, the danger he faced was real.

FAST FACTS

In 2005, Pistone cowrote a novel, *The Good Guys*, with Salvatore "Bill" Bonanno, a member of the crime family Pistone had infiltrated in the 1970s and 1980s.

He explains his attitude toward that danger in his book:

> Before the first trial began, we had definite word of a hit contract out on my life. . . . The federal prosecutors petitioned the court to allow me and another agent I had worked with during the final year to withhold our real names when testifying. . . . But [Judge Robert W. Sweet] denied our motion because of constitutional rights of defendants to confront their accusers. I felt neither betrayed nor surprised. There were never any guarantees.

Pistone spent the next several years testifying in various trials. In fact, he spent nearly as much time testifying as he had spent undercover. Eventually, his work finished, Pistone resigned from the FBI. He and his family changed their names, and he moved to another part of the country to start a new life. He had done amazing work.

Joseph Valachi became a member of the Mafia around 1930. He was a good soldier, doing what his bosses told him to do. One day, though, Valachi got caught selling drugs. While in prison, Valachi began to think that his boss, Vito Genovese, had ordered to have him killed. In prison, Valachi killed a man he believed was ready to kill him.

A headline in the New York *Daily Mirror* proclaims "Valachi Sings Here Today." The headline refers to the testimony, in 1963, of mob figure Joe Valachi, shown right at the time of his appearance before a Senate committee on organized crime. Valachi was the first member of the mob to ever publicly acknowledge the existence of the Mafia.

Ready to Talk

Valachi knew that he faced a death sentence for the murder. So he decided to talk. He asked authorities to give him a lighter sentence—serving life in prison rather than a death sentence—in exchange for everything he could tell them about the Mafia.

Over eight months starting in late 1962, FBI agent James Flynn interviewed Valachi. The next year, Valachi came to tell members of Congress what he knew. He talked about several crime families that controlled crime in and around New York.

Valachi said that 12 of the most powerful crime bosses controlled crime across the country. For the first time in more than 40 years, an insider was telling the truth about the Mafia. Valachi's words stunned lawmakers.

They also had a huge impact on the FBI. Valachi's words pushed the FBI—to continue facing up to the reality of organized crime, and then to go after the mob itself.

Defining Organized Crime

Organized crime is any large, complex network of criminals who work together committing crimes. In one sense, organized crime is like a business: its goal is to make money. But organized crime means making that money in criminal ways. These criminals sell illegal drugs, run **prostitution** rings, or manage illegal gambling. They use extortion to force honest people to pay them money. They bribe public officials to leave them alone.

Organized crime is also brutal. These criminals are willing to kill anyone who gets in their way.

YOU DON'T HAVE TO BE ITALIAN . . .

Books and movies make it seem that only Italian Americans are involved in organized crime. It is true that many crime families are filled with Italian Americans. They are part of the network long called the Mafia or **La Cosa Nostra**. But many other ethnic groups have been involved in organized crime—both in the past and today. No group has a monopoly on crime.

Many groups have had their own version of the Mafia. Historically, mobsters were often tied to ethnic communities, neighborhoods, and immigrant groups. Shown here are (top row and bottom left) Jewish-American mobsters Arnold Rothstein (gambling; behind the "fixing" of the 1919 World Series, in which some Chicago White Sox players deliberately lost to the Cincinnati Reds), Meyer Lansky (gambling; basis for various movie gangsters), Benjamin "Bugsy" Siegel (gambling), and Louis "Lepke" Buchalter (narcotics and contract killings; shown handcuffed to Bureau director J. Edgar Hoover, left); and Irish-American mobsters Jack "Legs" Diamond (**bootlegging**) and James "Whitey" Bulger (extortion, narcotics, money laundering; on the FBI's Ten Most Wanted list of fugitives).

Gangsters of the 1920s and 1930s

Criminal gangs became a major problem in the 1920s. This was especially true during a period known as **Prohibition**, which lasted from 1920 to 1933. During Prohibition, it was illegal to sell alcoholic beverages. Criminal gangs smuggled liquor into the country illegally from Canada and made large amounts of money by selling illegal drinks in secret bars called speakeasies.

With no one willing to testify against notorious Chicago gangster Al Capone (above), the government finally convicted him of income tax evasion.

One center of this gang activity was Chicago. There, much of the activity was led by Al Capone and others. Local and state authorities did nothing to stop Capone. For years, federal officials could not get anyone to give evidence against him.

Eventually, federal officials charged Capone with failing to pay his income taxes. Agents of the U.S. Treasury Department, who enforce tax laws, did the main work against Capone. The FBI mostly watched, although agents did arrest Capone at one point for **contempt of court**. He served a few months in prison for this crime.

The FBI did catch several notorious gangsters in the 1930s. These criminals generally had small gangs that roamed from state to state robbing banks. They were not really organized crime gangs.

Meanwhile, the Mafia grew. New York mobster Lucky Luciano organized a network that united mobsters around the country. They cooperated with each other—as long as nobody invaded another boss's territory.

Organized Crime Grows

Over time, crime organizations found new ways of earning money. When Nevada made gambling legal, mobsters built casinos in Las Vegas. They also ran casinos in Cuba. Some criminal leaders, like Meyer Lansky, worried that they might be charged with avoiding income taxes, just as Capone had been. So they started

The Untouchables was a 1960s TV series based on a true-life group of agents in the 1920s and 1930s. The agents, led by Eliot Ness (played by Robert Stack, shown pointing), were often thought to be FBI agents. They actually worked for the U.S. Treasury Department. One of their primary Prohibition-era targets was Chicago mobster Al Capone.

money laundering operations to hide their money. They also opened bank accounts in other countries.

For a long time, the FBI did nothing to go after organized crime. One reason was that these gangs typically broke state, not federal, laws. Also, FBI Director J. Edgar Hoover denied that there was anything like an organized crime network that spanned the nation, adding that any such

Charles "Lucky" Luciano is shown here in a 1936 New York Police Department mug shot. Luciano forged associations and alliances with various factions, families, and bosses within organized crime. He conducted much of his mob business from outside the United States, in Cuba and Italy.

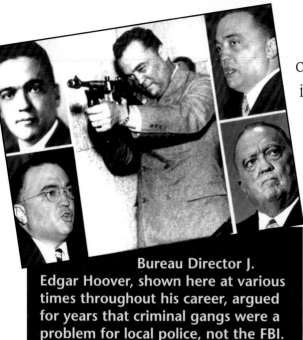

Bureau Director J. Edgar Hoover, shown here at various times throughout his career, argued for years that criminal gangs were a problem for local police, not the FBI.

claim was "baloney." "No single individual or [group] of **racketeers** [criminals] dominates organized crime across the country," Hoover declared.

Critics say that Hoover was just making excuses. They say that organized gangs crossed state lines, making their actions federal crimes. They claim that Hoover avoided investigating the mob because it would take too long. He was interested in making lots of arrests as quickly as possible to show that his Bureau was worth the money it was receiving. The lack of a guaranteed success, say critics, convinced Hoover to leave organized crime alone.

Growing Spotlight on Organized Crime

The situation began to change in 1957. On November 14, a sergeant of the New York state police was patrolling a rural area in the state. He was startled to see several black limousines all heading to the same home in the small community of Apalachin. The state trooper—named Edgar Croswell— knew that the man whose home they were visiting had been arrested several times.

Suspicious, Croswell set up a roadblock and called for help. When news of the barricades reached the men attending the meeting, they began to scatter. Croswell and his fellow troopers nabbed several of the men and got the names of many more. They realized that more than 60 leading crime figures had been at the meeting. They included crime bosses from New York, Cleveland, San Francisco, Milwaukee, Los Angeles, Denver, Buffalo, Chicago, Dallas, and Miami.

FAST FACTS

The Mafia earned an estimated $500 million in 1945. In 1965, that sum had shot up to $40 billion. By 1985, its illegal earnings were thought to have reached $100 billion.

The meeting generated lots of publicity. Police officials were asked embarrassing questions. Hoover and the FBI received criticism. The Apalachin meeting spurred the Bureau to move.

Hoover took two steps. First, he told all field offices to begin tracking the 10 leading organized crime figures in its area. This "Top Hoodlum Program" aimed mainly at gathering **intelligence** by monitoring the crime bosses and learning what they were up to. Agents secretly used some illegal methods, including **wiretaps**, to get this information.

The second step was information gathering of another kind. Hoover asked the Bureau's research section to look into the issue of organized crime. A year later, it produced a report that convinced Hoover that nationwide crime organizations did, indeed, exist. He refused to make the report public, however.

New Information

In 1961, John F. Kennedy became president. He named his brother Robert F. Kennedy as attorney general, which put him in charge of the FBI. Robert Kennedy wanted to push the FBI to

JCTURE OF A MOB FAMILY

sa Nostra is divided into several large
s called "families." Each family is
control of criminal operations in a
n geographical area. The families all
a similar structure:

The *boss*, also called "the don," is at
the top. The boss is chosen by vote of
the capos, or "captains."

The *underboss* is the second-in-
command. A boss might have two or
three of these aides, but many
families only have one.

The *consigliere*, or "counselor," is an
advisor to the boss. This person is
often the one who works out agree-
ments with the bosses of other
families.

The *capos* (short for *caporegimes*), or
"captains," are the four to nine
leaders who directly control the men
who do the gang's work. The boss
gives them their posts, and they must
show loyalty. If not, they will be killed.

Soldiers are the lowest-ranking
members of the gang. Groups of six to
ten soldiers serve under each capo.
Those soldiers who have killed someone on the orders of higher-ups are
called "made men."

Associates are not fully members of
the family. They are invited to help
the family carry out its activities but
are not yet fully accepted. Only after
they prove themselves over time can
they become soldiers.

move harder and faster
against organized crime.
He favored passing a
law that would make
wiretaps legal. He also
pushed the FBI to move
harder against organized
crime—especially after
Joseph Valachi spoke at
hearings before
Congress in 1963.

Valachi's words gave
FBI Director Hoover a
chance to avoid embar-
rassment. For years,
Hoover had denied that
there was such as thing
as "the Mafia." In his
testimony, Valachi said
that the people in
organized crime called
their crime families *La
Cosa Nostra* ("our thing"
in Italian). Hoover was
able to declare that—as
he had said all along—
there is no Mafia. But
he vowed that the FBI
would go after this

new crime machine, La Cosa Nostra. From then on, FBI documents always called the Italian American mob the "LCN," or La Cosa Nostra.

Wayne Comer was once one of the top agents in the Philadelphia field office, and he later became an instructor at the FBI Academy. He believed that it was external pressure that pushed the Bureau to go after the Mafia. He told journalist Ronald Kessler, "If it weren't for the trooper in New York and Valachi, we never would have gotten into organized crime."

Fits and Starts

In the 1960s, the FBI took some steps to try to go after mobsters. They had mixed success.

The Chicago field office got lucky when one of its telephone bugs allowed agents to overhear a crime boss talking about other crime figures. Soon more bugs were in place, and more information was gathered. But the Bureau could not arrest these crime bosses because the wiretaps were still illegal. Evidence the FBI obtained through the wiretaps could not be used in court.

The Buffalo, New York, field office managed to arrest several bookmakers linked to the Mafia family there. The **bookmakers** received only light sentences, however. Later, the Buffalo agents identified a bookmaker who had ties to bookies in cities across the country, from Miami and Cleveland to Las Vegas and Los Angeles. On March 1, 1968, FBI agents in several cities arrested bookies. Once again, however, the criminals received only light sentences.

At times the Bureau stumbled in its efforts against the mob, too. Chicago agents tailed Sam Giancana, a crime boss in that city. They followed him so closely that Giancana became aware of their surveillance. Annoyed, he filed a lawsuit demanding that the FBI stop watching him. The judge agreed with Giancana, calling the FBI's behavior "harassment" and "an admission of ineptness" of earlier surveillance methods. He ordered the Bureau to show more restraint.

The Justice Department had problems of its own. Attorney General Robert Kennedy had set up special teams of lawyers to go after crime figures. The group won some **convictions**, but most of these convictions were only for minor offenses. Without a new Joe Valachi to give evidence against crime bosses, the crime families remained intact.

Targeting the Mafia

Meanwhile, Lyndon B. Johnson had become president of the United States following the assassination of John F. Kennedy in 1963. He ordered a top-level commission to look into the problem of crime and law enforcement. In 1967, the commission issued its report. The report placed La Cosa Nostra at the center of organized crime:

> The core of organized crime in the United States consists of 24 groups operating criminal cartels [closed organizations] in large cities across the nation. Their membership is exclusively Italian, they are in

Chicago crime boss Sam Giancana is shown in June 1974 as he entered the federal building in Chicago. Giancana argued successfully that the FBI's constant surveillance of him constituted harassment.

frequent communication with each other, and their smooth functioning is insured by a national body of overseers.

The commission urged the United States Congress to pass new laws to help the FBI and police crack down on this criminal network. Congress did pass new laws in 1968 and 1970 that gave the Bureau and police forces powerful tools against organized crime. A 1968 crime law gave the FBI the power to install wiretaps with a judge's approval. Now the Bureau could listen to mobsters' conversations as they planned crimes, and use the evidence in court.

Two laws passed in 1970 also gave the FBI weapons to use against La Cosa Nostra. The Organized Crime Control Act created a witness protection program. Under this program, mobsters who testified in court against other gangsters would be protected. The government promised to give them—and their wives and children—new identities and to move them to another part of the country. The law made it possible to persuade **informants** to speak openly and honestly in court without fear of being killed.

The other 1970 law was the Racketeer Influenced and Corrupt Organizations (RICO) Act. This law made any business illegal if it was funded by money obtained through crimes. The tough law also gave the government the power to seize money or property that had been earned through crime.

By 1970, the FBI was in a better position to move against organized crime. It was gaining the intelligence it needed, and the tough new laws gave it powerful weapons. Soon, the Bureau would pounce.

3 Later Successes

For about six years in the 1970s and 1980s, FBI agents worked hard to break a major organized crime case. They called this case "the Pizza Connection." The funny name hid a serious set of crimes.

Slicing Up the Pizza Connection

Mob figures used pizza restaurants to hide their sale of illegal drugs. The American mobsters worked closely with members of Italy's Mafia, who supplied the drugs. The operation covered six states from New York to Wisconsin and brought in more than 300 pounds (135 kilograms) of heroin each year.

Tommaso Buscetta (holding blanket), a high-ranking Mafia boss in Sicily, Italy, is shown being helped off a plane in Rome. Buscetta was one of the first insiders to give key evidence against the mob. His testimony in the famed "Pizza Connection" trial helped put hundreds of mobsters in the United States and Italy in prison.

Each yearly haul could sell for as much as $1.6 billion on the street. The first clues to this network came through the undercover work of Joe Pistone.

Finally, in 1984, the Justice Department had enough evidence to bring charges. It issued indictments against 31 different people. Among these people were a leader of the Sicilian Mafia and Salvatore Catalano, a member of New York's Bonanno crime family. A year later, the trial began. Some of the original defendants were not tried. They had either died or were being held in other countries. Twenty-two went to trial, however.

The case was so complex that the trial lasted nearly a year and a half. Prosecutors questioned hundreds of witnesses and gave the jury thousands of documents showing the finances of the crime ring. They brought in evidence from hours of wiretapped conversations, but in an unusual way. Rather than reading the transcripts to jurors, the prosecutors had actors read the lines that the mobsters had spoken on the phone.

Four of the accused pleaded guilty, and one died during the trial. On March 2, 1987, the remaining 17 defendants were found guilty. The FBI had done its job.

Successes in Buffalo and Cleveland

The Buffalo field office enjoyed some success in its fight against the mob in the early 1970s. The new tools—in the form of the laws passed by Congress—were a great help. In 1972, agents there caught the local underboss committing **perjury**, or lying in court. He was sentenced to five years in prison. Later that year, the testimony of an FBI informant led to the conviction of a Buffalo capo and another mobster. The mobsters received stiff sentences: the capo was sentenced to 111 years, and the other mobster was sentenced to 80 years.

The Cleveland field office also had great success—though it was a long time coming. In the late 1970s, agents there found enough evidence to win indictments against five high-ranking Mafia members. The charges—based on RICO— were for murder and **bribery**. Prosecutors did not bring the case to trial for many years, however. Not until 1982 were the five men tried. Hours of wiretapped conversations and the testimony of an informant won convictions. Each man was sentenced to more than a dozen years in prison.

"Jimmy the Weasel" Fratianno, shown here during a murder trial in California, became a mob boss in Cleveland and Los Angeles in the 1970s and 1980s. When he learned that a contract had been put out on his life by rivals within his own organization, he became a federal informant. At the time, he was the second (following Joe Valachi) and highest-ranking mobster to turn on his crime family.

The same informant—"Jimmy the Weasel" Fratianno—was later used to secure the guilt of a family boss in northern New York. Later, his testimony won convictions against several members of the Los Angeles mob family.

The Mob and the Unions

One challenge that organized crime presented the FBI was fighting the control that crime families had gotten over several labor unions. Mobsters used threats, bribes, and extortion to rig union elections and make union officials do as they wanted.

The FBI had some early success with some

A HIGH PRICE TO PAY FOR JUSTICE

The Pizza Connection trials in New York City were matched by other trials in Italy. There, Judge Giovanni Falcone (left) was successful in pursuing the Sicilian Mafia. The trials put more than 300 criminals in prison.

Judge Falcone knew that he might have to pay a price for this work. And, eventually, the Sicilian mob did catch up with him. Mobsters planted a bomb that exploded near the judge's car. Falcone, his wife, and three other people were killed.

Louis Freeh (left) had worked closely with Falcone during the two sets of trials. As director of the FBI in the 1990s, Freeh wanted to pay tribute to the slain judge. He had a statue of Falcone placed at the FBI Academy in Quantico, Virginia. In dedicating the statue, Freeh paid tribute to Falcone: "Here was a judge . . . who made a deeply personal decision to enforce the law with all of its . . . strength—knowing full well that this commitment would place his very life in danger."

Teamsters union head James "Jimmy" Hoffa was convicted in 1964 of attempting to bribe a grand jury member. He was released from prison in 1971, and in 1975 he disappeared in suburban Detroit. He had been scheduled to meet with Mafia leaders at a local restaurant. For years, many theories have arisen about his connections with organized crime and his disappearance and supposed death at the hands of the mob.

of these cases. A 1978 Miami case produced charges against nearly two dozen union and business leaders for illegal payments. One of the union leaders was an organized crime figure. Another union case took place in Louisiana. That case eventually led to convictions of both the supposed head of La Cosa Nostra in New Orleans and a high-ranking state official.

The FBI worked hard to expose organized crime connections to the Teamsters International union. For many years, that union had been plagued by mob influence. The FBI code-named the investigation "Liberatus." In 1988, federal officials filed a lawsuit against Teamsters officials. The suit was based on information the FBI had gathered, and it charged that union leaders were controlled by organized crime. A year later, the union settled the suit by agreeing to let an outside group watch over its elections and its operations.

Over the years, the FBI has weakened mob control of this union in other ways. Among these, it has produced information leading to convictions of many Teamster officials.

The Commission Case

About the same time that the Pizza Connection case began, an even bigger case hit the Mafia. In February 1985, prosecutors announced charges against eight crime family members. They were charged with acting as the "Commission," the high council that controlled all La Cosa Nostra activity across the country. Armed with the RICO law, prosecutors said that these eight leaders had organized illegal financial dealings, ordered murders, and led crime bosses in other crimes.

The eight included the heads of three of the biggest crime families in New York City. They were Anthony Salerno, of the Genovese family; Anthony Corallo, of the Lucchese family; and Carmine Persico, of the Colombo family. Others charged included underbosses and counselors.

The trial lasted only 10 weeks. Once again, FBI wiretaps were key pieces of evidence. So, too, were surveillance photos taken by agents. Prosecutors got a perfect score—eight convictions. The judge sentenced seven of the eight men to 100 years in prison.

The Pizza Connection and Commission cases shook La Cosa Nostra. The mobsters knew the FBI was after them.

Anthony "Fat Tony" Salerno is shown here in a 1959 mug shot. Salerno worked his way to the top of the Genovese crime family by 1985, when the FBI arrested him and other New York crime bosses in the Commission case.

The Patriarca Case

New York City had many of the nation's 24 crime families. For that reason, much of the action against organized crime took place there. But there were La Cosa Nostra gangs in other cities, and they were targets, too.

In 1990, prosecutors brought charges in Boston against 21 members of the Patriarca crime family. Among those charged were two rival leaders, Raymond Patriarca and Nicholas Blanco.

Once again, the RICO law proved to be a key to bringing the charges, and wiretapped conversations helped convict the criminals. Some of the accused pleaded guilty. All the rest were found guilty as charged. It was another strong blow against organized crime.

Getting the "Dapper Don"

Always well dressed, John Gotti had earned the nickname "the Dapper Don." His natty appearance hid a ruthless interior. Gotti became the head of New York's Gambino crime family late in 1985 by a simple method. He had the current head of the family, Paul Castellano, murdered as Castellano was eating his dinner.

Gotti had another nickname. He was also called "the Teflon Don." This nickname referred to a nonstick coating given to pots and pans. Although police arrested Gotti three times (in 1986, 1987, and 1990), juries failed to convict him each time. Authorities could not get the charges to stick.

A new investigation—and a big break—changed that. Gotti was arrested once again in 1990 and charged with several crimes. They included murder, **conspiracy** to commit murder, racket-eering, **jury tampering**, gambling, and income tax evasion. This time, prosecu-tors had hours of wiretaps. They also had a special witness. Gotti's second in command, Salvatore "Sammy the Bull" Gravano, testified against his boss to save his own skin.

The trial began in the spring of 1992. Gotti's lawyers tried to convince the jury that they should doubt Gravano's word since he was just trying to save himself. The jury disagreed. On April 2, 1992, they found him guilty of every charge. The head of the FBI field office in

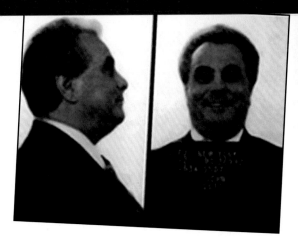

The body of crime boss Paul Castellano lies on a stretcher outside a steak house in New York after he was gunned down in December 1985. John Gotti (shown below in a mug shot) took over the Gambino family following the shooting.

MOVING ON TO BIGGER THINGS

Federal prosecutors who were successful against the mob often gained fame from their victories. Some also went on to bigger jobs. The prosecutor who worked the Pizza Connection case was Louis J. Freeh. He became director of the FBI in 1993.

Rudolph Giuliani (shown below in 1984) was the prosecutor in the Commission Case. In large part because of his success as a prosecutor, he was elected mayor of New York City in 1993.

New York City was jubilant. "The Teflon Don is covered with Velcro," he said, "and every charge stuck."

After catching Gotti, the FBI continued to investigate the Gambino crime family. Over the next several years, prosecutors succeeded in convicting more than 200 members of the Gambino organization. The FBI even arrested the boss's son, John Gotti, Jr., twice. The younger Gotti was able to escape conviction, however, just as his father had done for so many years.

Recent Wins

From 2002 to 2004, more than 70 members of the Bonanno family were prosecuted. Joseph Massino, the Bonanno boss, was sentenced to life in prison for a host of crimes, including seven murders. He managed to escape a death sentence, however, only because he agreed to talk to the FBI.

The FBI is still working against the mob. In 2008, the Bureau struck at the Gambino family once again. In a coordinated assault, agents throughout New York City and neighboring areas arrested dozens of members of the family on the same day. The suspects included John D'Amico, thought to be the boss of the family at the time. By summer, all but two of the defendants had pleaded guilty. James Walden, who had prosecuted cases against the

FBI agents and members of the NYPD are shown in what the FBI billed as a "Mafia takedown" of organized crime members in February 2008. The coordinated crackdown resulted in the arrests of 62 members of the Gambino, Genovese, and Bonanno families.

Bonanno family, praised the action. "They essentially took out the entire organization in one fell swoop," he said.

The Pantheon Project

In the last three decades, the FBI has enjoyed great success going after La Cosa Nostra members and leaders. Many crime families have been broken. The FBI continues to work against crime organizations, however.

Some of those efforts are international. Two different programs help FBI agents work closely with police in Italy, home of the Sicilian Mafia. In the Pantheon Project, FBI agents and Italian police are sent to each other's countries. They work closely with the home law enforcement officers to help break crime rings that span borders. The Italian-American Working Group is a meeting held every year. At these sessions, FBI agents and Italian police share information and make plans for coming operations.

CHAPTER 4 Sticky Business

FBI undercover agent Joe Pistone ("Donnie Brasco") walked a fine line when he posed as a mobster and entered the Bonanno family. He was careful to remember what he was—an FBI agent doing his job.

Showing Just the Right Amount of Respect

While Joe Pistone gained a certain amount of respect for the mobsters he knew best, he always kept in mind that he was a law enforcement officer and they were criminals. In his book, when describing the days just before he left the undercover life, he discusses his views of his partner, Benjamin "Lefty" Ruggiero, and his capo, Dominick "Sonny Black" Napolitano:

> I knew that both Lefty and Sonny loved me in their own ways. Either would have killed me in a minute. . . . The difference between our worlds was that I wouldn't kill them. I would just put them in the can [prison]. . . . Nothing I did in my job was affected by any feelings I had for Sonny or anybody else. That was my discipline. . . . You can't have those personal feelings in this business. I was not there to be buddy-buddy with these guys. I would not allow myself to become that emotionally attached.

Benjamin "Lefty" Ruggiero is shown in an FBI surveillance photograph. The photo was taken as Ruggiero was leaving a social club, moments after he had learned that his partner in crime, Donnie Brasco, was in reality FBI undercover agent Joe Pistone.

Pistone's discipline helped him survive—and send dozens of mobsters to prison. His success convinced the FBI to try other undercover operations to break other mob families. Having inside information gave the FBI a powerful lever to pry open the secret operations of organized crime gangs. But living the life of a criminal also exposed undercover agents—and the FBI itself—to dangers. Those dangers were not only the threat of death if the undercover man was discovered. There was also the possibility that the agent, and the Bureau, could become corrupted.

Growing Too Close?

In 1975, FBI agent Joe Connolly met with Boston mobster James "Whitey" Bulger. Connolly had a proposal. He wanted Bulger to cooperate with the FBI by revealing secrets that the Bureau could use to catch other gangsters. In return, the Bureau would ignore any crimes committed by Bulger and his partner, Stephen "The Rifleman" Flemmi, might commit—short

Boston gangster James "Whitey" Bulger (right), was a prominent figure in organized crime throughout New England. In 1975, he became an informant for the FBI following a meeting with agent Joe Connolly. For years, Bulger and his cohort, Stephen "The Rifleman" Flemmi (shown in a surveillance photo below), enjoyed a privileged relationship with the FBI. Protected from prosecution as informants, they continued their life of crime. Finally, the FBI gathered enough evidence to bring charges against them. Bulger, warned by agent Connolly of the impending charges, fled. Bulger has been a fugitive since 1995.

WANTED
BY THE FBI
FOR RICO, EXTORTION
JAMES J. BULGER
AKA WHITEY BULGER

DOB:	9/3/29
POB:	Boston, MA
HEIGHT:	5'7"
WEIGHT:	150 lbs.
BUILD:	Medium
RACE:	White
SEX:	Male
HAIR:	Silver/White
EYES:	Blue

ALIASES: • Whitey Bulger • Jimmy Boy • Thomas Baxter • Tom Harris

Bulger, a major organized crime figure in Boston, MA is being sought for extortion and RICO charges. Bulger has funded his activities through the extortion of illegitimate criminal operations to include gambling, loan-sharking and drugs.

Warrant Information: A federal warrant was issued on January 4, 1995 in Boston, MA charging Bulger with Extortion and RICO.

Anyone having information regarding Bulger should notify the Federal Bureau of Investigation Violent Fugitive Task Force at Boston, Massachusetts, (617) 742-5533 or the nearest FBI Office.

BULGER SHOULD BE CONSIDERED ARMED AND DANGEROUS
CALLERS MAY REMAIN ANONYMOUS
(617)742-5533

$250,000 REWARD

of murder. Bulger did not agree right away. Still, the idea appealed to him. "You can't survive without friends in law enforcement," he told Connolly. Two weeks later, the two men made the deal final.

Connolly had grown up in the same neighborhood as Bulger and had known the criminal as a child. Perhaps his closeness to Bulger clouded his judgment. Perhaps he lost his good sense because of the successes the Bureau enjoyed as a result of the connection. Bulger did indeed give good information to Connolly.

Tips from Bulger helped the FBI move against the Italian-American Mafia in the city. They used his information to win a court order allowing them to place microphones in a building that served as the Mafia's headquarters. That bug gave the Bureau enough evidence to win a few dozen convictions.

FAST FACTS

As of 2009, James "Whitey" Bulger was still at large. The FBI reward for information about him—which had initially been $500,000—was upped to $1 million and later to $2 million.

Covering up Crimes?

Meanwhile, though, Bulger's Irish Mafia grew in power. Other law enforcement officers in the Boston area received evidence and tips that Bulger was expanding his own criminal operation. They heard of murders that he and Flemmi had committed. However, Connolly stepped over the line to protect his source of information about the Italian mob. He moved to block investigations or downplayed Bulger's involvement in crimes.

The cover-up went farther. John Morris was the head of the organized crime squad in the Boston field office. Connolly worked under him. Years later, Morris admitted that he had warned Bulger about a police effort to bug the mobster. He also admitted taking payments from Bulger. Years later, Flemmi swore under oath that the FBI gave Bulger and him tips on several occasions of impending arrests. The two gangsters used that information to warn the suspects to flee.

Agent Bob Fitzpatrick, who had worked as a top-ranking member of the Boston field office, explained the problem to a reporter who investigated the matter. "You can never have the top guy [Bulger] as an informant. You have the top guy, he's making policy [decisions], and then he owns you. He owns you!" He added, "The FBI is being used."

The Aftermath

In 1988, the *Boston Globe* ran a four-part story about Bulger and his brother, a prominent Massachusetts politician. In that story, the reporters discussed the "special relationship" that Whitey Bulger seemed to have with the FBI. The story included statements by local FBI officials denying any wrongdoing. Still, the story was the beginning of the end.

Eventually, the truth came out. Connolly retired from the Bureau in 1990. Morris was transferred to other posts. New agents and prosecutors came to town, and they were determined to go after Bulger. In 1995, these investigators had enough information to indict Bulger and Flemmi. Bulger—warned by Connolly—fled the area before he could be arrested. Flemmi was arrested, tried, and convicted.

Over the years, more charges were added to Bulger's list of crimes, including 19 murders. The FBI placed him on the Ten Most Wanted List. He still eluded justice.

Connolly was not so lucky. Based on what Flemmi said, Connolly was arrested in 1999 and charged with several crimes. He was found guilty in 2002 and sent to prison for 10 years. Since being sent to prison, he has also been charged with being involved in the 1982 murder of a man

PAYING FOR MISTAKES

At least once, the federal government had to pay dearly for its mistakes. In 1968, Joseph Barboza identified four men as carrying out the killing of a minor criminal named Edward Deegan three years before. The four were Peter Limone, Joseph Salvati, Louis Greco, and Henry Tameleo. There were two problems with Barboza's testimony. First, someone else had done the crime. And second, the FBI knew that, but the real killer was an FBI inform-ant, and the Bureau let Barboza testify anyway.

In 2001, the full details were brought to light. A Massachusetts judge overturned the four convictions. The decision did not help Tameleo and Greco—they had already died in prison, in 1985 and 1995, respectively.

In 2007, Limone, Salvati, and the families of the two others sued the United States government. That July, Judge Nancy Gertner ruled in their favor. She awarded the men and their families $101.7 million in damages. She also sharply criticized the FBI for framing the four men. After the verdict, Limone told reporters, "I thank this court for mak-ing a terrible wrong a right. I hope this never happens to anyone again."

Joseph Salvati (left) and Peter Limone embrace outside the Federal Courthouse in Boston in July 2007. they had just been awarded a $101.7 million settlement for their wrongful conviction and three decades of imprisonment. The two men were released from prison in 2001 after it was learned the FBI withheld who was going to give evidence against Bulger. Connolly was charged with warning Bulger about this danger, which led Bulger to order the man's death. Once again, Flemmi would be a key witness against him.

Former FBI agent John J. Connolly, Jr., is shown in 2002 entering Boston federal court, where he faced charges related to his handling of informants James "Whitey" Bulger and Stephen "The Rifleman" Flemmi. Connolly's case is an example of the risks taken by agencies such as the FBI when they become too attached to criminal informants.

Other Problems

The FBI had other problems as a result of working so closely with criminals. In using informants, they had to rely on criminals. Those criminals clearly helped the government's cause when they testified against their former partners and bosses. But they could not necessarily be counted on to live an honest life afterward.

One such mobster, Joe Barboza, helped bring down the Patriarca family of New England. He entered the witness protection program and tried to live a legal life—for a while. Soon, though, he was selling drugs, and soon after that he was back in prison. After his release, he moved to San Francisco and lived by extortion. His life of crime ended only when he was shot dead.

"Sammy the Bull" Gravano was another mobster who could not escape lifelong habits of crime. After

Salvatore "Sammy the Bull" Gravano is shown in 1993 before a Senate subcommittee investigating organized crime. His testimony helped send Gambino mob family boss John Gotti to prison. Gravano entered the witness protection program, but he later returned to his own life of crime and was sentenced to prison in 2002 for masterminding a drug ring.

helping put John Gotti in prison, Gravano also went into the witness protection program. He was moved to the Phoenix, Arizona, area, where he started dealing in drugs. He, too, was arrested again.

Critics say that the witness protection program is flawed. Criminals can use it to keep themselves out of prison—and use government-supplied money to launch new lives of crime. Crime scholar Michael Woodiwiss points to another problem— paying informants. Woodiwiss says that this practice leads to "informing for profit." He explains: "Informants can now receive a salary and bonuses for information, whether or not it leads to convictions."

CHAPTER 5
Organized Crime Goes International

Late in 2004, two members of a Russian organized-crime gang decided on a surefire way to make money. They planned to kill businessmen Slava and Alex Konstantinovsky, from Ukraine, and then take over their company. The criminals were Monya Elson and Leonid Roytman. A few months later, they began talking to a pair of men to carry out the deed, offering total of $100,000 for the murders.

Fur hats are sold illegally on a street in the Brighton Beach section of Brooklyn, New York. Brighton Beach is home to about 60,000 Russian immigrants. It is also the target of FBI investigations into organized crime activity generated by the Russian mob in the United States and abroad.

A Pair of Untrustworthy Hit Men

The killers began taping the conversations, thinking that they would protect themselves from being blackmailed or killed later by the men hiring them. Finally, they went to Ukraine's police and offered their services—and the tapes—to the police.

Working with the help of the FBI and New York City police, Ukraine's police set up a trap. The killers pretended to have killed one of the brothers, whom the Ukraine police secretly hid. Then the killers demanded their payment. It was arranged to make the payment in New York City to an undercover officer. There, the two criminals were arrested. On the day the arrests were announced, Mark Mershon, one of the top officials of the FBI's New York field office, declared:

> "This is a case of two Russian mobsters who personify ruthlessness and cold-blooded greed. More importantly, it's also a case of solid teamwork between law enforcement agencies on opposite sides of the globe, joining forces to bring these men to justice."

Gambling with the Law

The FBI's war on La Cosa Nostra was a huge success. By the first decade of the 21st century, there were only about 1,150 members of the Mafia left. About two-thirds were in New York. Chicago had once had seven crime families; now it had but three. The Mafia was all but gone from Cleveland and other cities. Law professor G. Robert Blakey offered this judgment on the Mafia's fate: "Most families of the mob are today little more than street gangs."

The FBI's success against La Cosa Nostra was the good news. The bad news was that new groups continued to arise, and, as they did, they quickly grew powerful.

A case in the early 2000s showed how quickly other gangs moved in to fill the void. In 2001, agents in New York City began hearing about a new gang. They were Albanian Americans, and they called themselves "the Corporation." They had started as members of John Gotti's Gambino crime family but had moved out on their own in 1993. Eventually, they took over gambling operations in one area of New York City. Internationally, Albanian gangs are also known to be involved in the illegal gun and sex

FAST FACTS

In 2005, the FBI was carrying out more than 650 investigations into Italian American organized crime families. It had nearly 470 investigations into Asian and African organized crime gangs.

17th Annual International Asian Organized Crime Conference

Then-FBI Director Louis Freeh is shown addressing a conference on Asian organized crime in 1995. According to the FBI, the growth of the immigrant Asian population has made Asian organized crime more serious a problem than the Mafia, especially as Asian street gangs, like their counterparts in other ethnic communities, have become more organized and violent.

trades. In the 2009 movie *Taken*, the story revolves around Albanian mobsters who ruthlessly kidnap young women and girls and force them into sexual slavery.

The New York Albanian gang made its money through dozens of video poker machines. Investigators believe that they made as much as $1.8 million a year from each machine. In 2004, the FBI moved in and arrested 26 members of the gang. The lawyer who defended the leader, Alex "Allie Boy" Rudaj, protested that his client was innocent. "My client vehemently [strongly] denies the charges that he is some sort of mob king-pin," he told reporters. "He's a family man. He's got a wife and two children." Based on the FBI's evidence, the jury disagreed. It found Rudaj guilty, and he was sentenced to 27 years in prison for gambling and other crimes. The other accused pleaded guilty or were found guilty when they were put on trial.

Many Different Mobs

Today, going after organized crime means going after Russians, Japanese, Nigerians, Chinese, Israelis, Eastern Europeans, and South Americans, among others. Some of the crimes they commit

This FBI surveillance photograph shows Albanian-American mobster Alex Rudaj, boss of the Rudaj Organization, outside a bar in Queens, New York, in 2003. At least one FBI official has put the Rudaj Organization on a level with Mafia families in New York.

INTERPOL

One of the international groups that the FBI works with is Interpol. The official name of this group is the International Criminal Police Organization. Formed in 1923, Interpol has 186 nations as members.

Interpol specializes in the international drug trade, human trafficking, white-collar crime, and **terrorism**. It only becomes involved if several member nations are affected by the crime.

Interpol keeps a database of crimes and criminals. Police officials in member countries can tap into that database to find information they need. The FBI has a special group called the Office of International Operations (OIO) to handle contact with Interpol. Interpol also offers another benefit: it has a communications office that makes it easy for law enforcement officials in one country to contact those in another.

are **white-collar crimes**, such as **piracy**. This crime can include selling illegal versions of movies on DVD or selling fake designer clothes. Other criminal activities, like the drug trade, are part of more traditional organized crime. The various groups also carry out arms sales that threaten peace around the world.

These criminals not only have operations in their own countries. They also commit crimes in the United States. African groups have operations in several U.S. cities, from Washington, D.C., to Atlanta, Houston, and Milwaukee. Asian organized crime gangs are active in Honolulu and such West Coast cities as Portland, San Francisco, and Seattle. But they can also be found in Chicago, Detroit, and Philadelphia. Middle Eastern groups are most active in the states of New Jersey and New York in the east and in Ohio and Illinois in the Midwest. Russian mobsters are especially active in New York City, Los Angeles, San Francisco, and Miami, among other cities.

Organizing for the Fight

To combat these international criminals, the FBI needs international cooperation. It has special offices in more than 70 cities where agents coordinate their crime-fighting efforts with local officials. It maintains close ties to Interpol, the international police agency. The FBI has also joined with Australian law enforcement groups to start a police academy. Based in Thailand, the academy trains Asian police in crime-solving skills. Those police can then better cooperate with FBI agents.

FAST FACTS

The FBI took charge of security for the 1984 Olympics, held in Los Angeles, California. To prepare for the event, the agency created its Hostage Rescue Team in 1983. The team has since responded to many hostage situations.

The FBI has a special Organized Crime Section at its headquarters. That section is divided into three groups. One focuses on ongoing investigations of La Cosa Nostra. The other two concentrate on Eurasian/Middle Eastern organized crime gangs and on Asian and African organized crime.

In 2007, the FBI completed a review of the problem of international organized crime. It identified eight important threats from these criminals:

- Increased efforts to control energy resources
- Aid to terrorists and enemies of the United States
- Trafficking in humans and illegal goods, including drugs
- Corrupting U.S. and international finances

- Using the Internet to obtain information about U.S. citizens and engage in identify theft
- Using **fraudulent investments** to take money from Americans
- Corrupting public officials in other countries
- Using violence to gain and keep power

To combat these threats, the FBI has adopted a new strategy to fight international organized crime. One of its goals is to further increase FBI work with law enforcement in other countries.

Catching the Smugglers

A 2005 case showed how the FBI coordinates many different groups to investigate the operations of these international gangs. In August of that year, officials from the Justice Department, the FBI, the Department of Homeland Security, and other agencies announced the arrests of several individuals in an international drug **smuggling** and **counterfeiting** ring.

The arrests came as a result of two operations. One

In 2006, FBI Director Robert S. Mueller (left) awarded Italian National Police Chief Giovanni De Gennaro the FBI's Medal of Meritorious Achievement. As reported on the FBI's Web site, De Gennaro was honored "for his pivotal role in a decades-long relationship that initially targeted organized crime connections in the U.S. and Italy but that has evolved into a model of international law-enforcement cooperation."

of these, centered in New Jersey, was called Operation Royal Charm. The other, in Los Angeles, had the name Operation Smoking Dragon. Agents working on the two coasts had to coordinate their efforts. They also had to work with the U.S. Secret Service; the Bureau of Alcohol, Tobacco, Firearms, and Explosives; immigration officials; and the Postal Service inspection office. They even got help from state and local police and from the Royal Canadian Mounted Police.

The cooperation paid off. Prosecutors indicted nearly 90 people for the crimes. In making the arrests, agents seized $4.5 million in counterfeit money, along with drugs and counterfeit cigarettes.

Members of the Jackson, Mississippi, Police Department stand by as U.S. Secret Service agent Larry Rowlett (seated) explains U.S. Treasury Department markings on paper money. One purpose of this 1998 news conference was to announce the busting of the largest counterfeit money ring in Mississippi. Another was to publicize the successful results of cooperative ventures between local authorities and federal agencies.

6 Going After Gangs

Selling illegal drugs is highly profitable for whoever controls the trade. And drug use was on the rise in the 1970s and 1980s, giving drug dealers a growing demand for their illegal substances. For years, La Cosa Nostra had controlled the sale of illegal drugs in the United States. When the Mafia became weaker, other groups took control of the illegal drug trade.

A New Type of Gangster

In the 1980s, a street gang called El Rukn (also spelled *El Rukin*) grabbed a large share of Chicago's drug trade. The FBI wanted to break the gang but lacked someone willing to talk. The breakthrough came in 1985. Agents learned that several gang members wanted for murder were hiding in Cleveland. They arrested them—and found the weak link.

One of the men arrested was a high-ranking official in the gang, Anthony Sumner. Sumner agreed to talk in return for lighter charges against him. He revealed that the gang's leader, Jeff Fort, though in prison, was still directing its criminal activities. The FBI placed a tap on the prison phone and recorded Fort's conversations. The wily gang members spoke in code, however. It took several months to crack that code and figure out what was being said.

El Rukn, once one of Chicago's most notorious street gangs, converted this former movie theater into a temple and used it as its headquarters in the 1980s. The FBI, along with other law enforcement agencies and neighborhood groups, has targeted street gangs that have brought the drug trade into many urban neighborhoods.

Eventually, agents learned that gang members were speaking to officials in the country of Libya. In return for money paid by the Libyan government, gang members agreed to blow up a U.S. commercial jet. To carry out its plan, the gang needed to buy a missile launcher. The FBI decided to trick them. Agents posed as arms dealers ready to sell such a weapon. After the sale, the FBI tracked the gang members back to their headquarters. A few days later, they closed in and arrested their suspects, who included leaders of the gang. The operation had weakened El Rukn—and prevented a terrorist attack.

The Drugs and Gangs Connection

Street gangs started to become a major problem in the 1980s when crack cocaine began to flood U.S. cities. Gang members took control of the profitable sale of this powerful drug. In 1997, Steven Wiley described the result to Congress. At the time, Wiley was head of the FBI's Violent Crimes and Major Offenders Section. The rise of crack, Wiley said, meant that

Many street gangs have achieved a level of organization and influence rivaling that of the mob. As the range of gang activity has grown, the need for cooperation between the FBI, local, state, and other federal law enforcement groups, and even international police agencies, has also increased.

. . . almost overnight a major industry was born, with major outlets in every neighborhood, tens of thousands of potential new customers and thousands of sales jobs available. In slightly over a decade, street gangs have become highly involved in drug trafficking at all levels.

In 2007, FBI director Robert S. Mueller told Congress just how serious he thought the gang problem was. He called organized gangs "a nationwide plague that is no longer limited to our largest cities."

WHY GANGS?

Why do people—especially young people—join gangs? Experts have identified five reasons:

- To give their lives some structure. Gangs have systems of rules and codes of behavior. By joining, young people find a system they can live by.
- To have a support network. Gang members support each other and care for each other. Of course, they also kill each other and commit crimes together. Young people in need of emotional comfort may ignore those negatives, however.
- To have a sense of belonging. People like to feel part of a group. Joining a gang satisfies that need for young people.
- To win economic gains. Gangs make money. Though their activities are illegal, gangs can give members the money they desire.
- To get excitement. The gang lifestyle can seem exciting and romantic to some young people. Unfortunately, it is also deadly dangerous.

A gang member in South Central Los Angeles is tended to by an officer after being wounded in a drive-by shooting. The glamour and excitement of gang life can quickly collide with reality in the face of violent injury and death.

Organized Efforts

Fighting gang crime has become a major goal of the FBI's efforts against organized crime. The Bureau estimates that as many as 800,000 people in the United States belong to some kind of gang.

The Bureau has responded to the problem of gangs with several efforts. In 1992, it launched the Safe Streets Violent Gang Initiative. That effort encouraged field offices to set up task forces that targeted gangs. Today, there are more than 170 of these task forces across the country.

The Bureau began another effort in 2005. Working with other law enforcement agencies, it set up the National Gang Intelligence Center. The center gathers data from around the country on gangs, their members, and their activities. FBI and state and local law enforcement officials can tap into the data to help them fight street gangs.

Another effort targets a specific street gang, called MS-13 (also known as *M-13*). According to the FBI, this gang operates in at least 42 states plus the District of Columbia. MS-13 is known for its high level of organization and for its particularly brutal acts of violence against those

An MS-13 suspect bearing gang tattoos is handcuffed and taken into custody. In 2004, the FBI created the MS-13 National Gang Task Force. A year later, the FBI helped create the National Gang Intelligence Center.

Suspected Mara Salvatrucha (MS-13) gang members are arrested by FBI and other law enforcement officers. Many MS-13 members are from El Salvador or are first-generation Salvadoran Americans. The gang also draws heavily from other Latin American immigrant groups.

whom it targets as its enemies. FBI investigators have found links between the gang and Mexico as well as countries in Central America. To help make the connections, the FBI has worked with police in those countries to share fingerprint records. The Bureau says the gang has more than 10,000 members in the United States. The work against this gang includes close cooperation with police in other countries.

Gaining Success

The FBI has had some success in its fight against street gangs. Gang arrests have taken place in cities from New York City to Tampa, Florida, to Chicago, to San Antonio, Texas, to San Diego. Even Keyser, West Virginia, was the scene of a large gang crackdown.

An operation in the Detroit area targeted a gang called the Chaldean Mafia. Made up of Iraqi Americans, the gang sold drugs in the Detroit area. The FBI investigation resulted in 111

One federal agent (far left) trains his gun on suspects as other officers raid a crack house. With so much gang activity associated with the sale of powerful, dangerous drugs, the FBI and other law enforcement agencies have focused on the illicit drug trade as a primary way of eradicating gang violence.

convictions and the seizure of $5.3 million and huge amounts of drugs.

The Boston field office struck against a gang called the Almighty Latin King/Queen Nation. This gang operated in several cities in Massachusetts. Several dozen members were indicted.

Nearly four dozen indictments were handed down against a Denver gang. Called the Gallant Knights Insane, this group was wanted for several violent crimes, including murders and robberies. When agents arrested the gang members, they secured not just weapons but also two bombs.

The Las Vegas field office joined with local police to go after the Rolling 60s Crips. This gang was involved in a violent conflict with rivals in the area. After 41 gang members were arrested, violent crime in the area dropped by 20 percent.

Memphis, Tennessee, was the scene of another drug-dealing gang, the Vice Lords. The FBI and other agencies seized more large amounts of cocaine and $2 million in cash. Nearly three dozen gang members were indicted.

Clearly, the weakening of the Mafia has not put an end to the FBI's fight against organized criminal activity. International crime and street gangs— once exclusively urban but now found in suburban and even rural areas—are but the latest fronts on the war against organized crime.

FAST FACTS

In 2001, the FBI investigations of gangs produced 2,168 convictions. The number of convictions ranged from near 1,700 to 1,964 a year over the next four years. In 2006, the Bureau had its most successful year to date with 2,199 convictions.

The graffiti tells a story. This wall is at a border point between rival gangs in Los Angeles. Because most street gangs fight their "turf" wars on the streets themselves, innocent bystanders are at far greater risk than when members of

CHRONOLOGY

1920: Prohibition begins; it lasts until 1933.

1929: Gangster Al Capone arrested for contempt of court by FBI agents.

1945: The Mafia earns an estimated $500 million.

1957: Meeting of several dozen organized crime figures in Apalachin, New York, on November 14.

FBI director J. Edgar Hoover orders field offices to start Top Hoodlum Program.

1958: FBI research section completes report stating that organized crime does exist and is a problem; Director Hoover agrees.

1961: Robert F. Kennedy becomes attorney general and pressures FBI to be more active against organized crime.

1962: FBI agent James Flynn begins his eight-month interview of Joseph Valachi.

1963: Joseph Valachi begins speaking to Congress on September 27.

1965: The Mafia earns an estimated $40 billion.

1967: President's Commission on Law Enforcement identifies 24 La Cosa Nostra families as the center of organized crime in the United States.

1968: FBI agents in several cities arrest Mafia-related bookmakers.

Congress passes Omnibus Crime Control and Safe Streets Act, giving the FBI the ability to use wiretaps to investigate organized crime.

1970: Organized Crime Council formed; it includes members of the attorney general's office and the heads of nine federal law enforcement agencies, including the FBI.

Organized Crime Control Act creates the federal witness protection program.

Racketeer Influenced and Corrupt Organizations (RICO) law is passed.

1975: Boston FBI agent Joe Connolly makes a deal with mobster James "Whitey" Bulger to work as an informant.

1976: FBI agent Joseph Pistone goes undercover as Donnie Brasco.

1985: Eight New York City mob figures are charged in the Commission Case in February.

Breakthrough in investigation of the Chicago gang El Rukn.

Trial in the Pizza Connection case begins.

The Mafia earns an estimated $100 billion.

1986: All eight accused in Commission Case are found guilty.

1987: Pizza Connection case ends in 17 convictions.

1988: FBI investigation code-named Liberatus results in suit filed against Teamsters union; Teamsters officials agree to allow outside supervision of elections.

1992: Mobster John Gotti convicted of murder and other charges.

FBI announces Safe Streets Violent Crimes

Initiative in an effort to stop gang violence.

1993: Louis J. Freeh becomes FBI director.

1995: FBI agent Joe Connolly warns mobster James "Whitey" Bulger that he is about to be arrested; Bulger flees.

2002: Beginning of more than five dozen trials against members of the Bonanno crime family.

2004: FBI arrests 26 members of the Albanian-American gang The Corporation.

FBI creates MS-13 National Gang Task Force.

2005: FBI arrests nearly 60 individuals in operations Royal Charm and Smoking Dragon.

FBI and other law enforcement agencies set up National Gang Intelligence Center.

2007: Department of Justice carries out study of international organized crime and develops new strategy to combat it.

2008: FBI agents arrest 62 members of Gambino crime family on a host of charges; 60 of them later plead guilty to various crimes.

GLOSSARY

bookmaker—a person who accepts illegal gambling bets. Bookmakers are also known as "bookies."

bootlegging—making or selling liquor illegally during Prohibition.

bribery—giving public officials money so they will act as you want them to.

conspiracy—a plot or an agreement to act together.

contempt of court—the crime of not cooperating in a trial by refusing to appear or to answer questions.

conviction—being found guilty in court for a crime.

counterfeiting—printing and circulating fake money.

extortion—the crime of forcing people to give you money by threatening to hurt them or their property if you do not.

fence—a person who deals in stolen goods, usually as a buyer.

fraudulent—fake; deceptive.

hearings—method used by Congress to investigate issues, in which people with knowledge on a matter answer questions.

indictment—document that formally and officially charges someone with a crime.

informant—someone with knowledge of a crime who cooperates with law enforcement officials by giving information about the crime and who committed it.

intelligence—information collected about possible threats or enemies.

investment—a plan people buy part of, using money they have saved, with the hopes of earning some regular income and seeing the value of the money invested grow.

jury tampering—illegally influencing members of a jury to vote in a specific way in deciding a trial.

La Cosa Nostra—another name for the Italian-American Mafia.

Mafia—name for the network of Italian-American crime organizations, also called La Cosa Nostra. The term "Mafia" has also been applied to organized crime networks run by other ethnic groups.

money laundering—processing stolen or dishonest money to conceal where it came from.

network—an interconnected chain, group, or system.

perjury—lying in a court of law.

piracy—selling goods of which the trademark, patent, or copyright is owned by someone else.

Prohibition—name for the period from 1920 to 1933 when the manufacture and distribution of alcohol was illegal.

prosecutor—government lawyer who brings cases in court against people charged with crimes.

prostitution—the crime of performing sex acts for money.

racketeer—another name for a member of an organized crime network; racketeering is a general name for the various crimes these groups commit.

smuggling—bringing goods or people into a country illegally.

surveillance—intense and often secret watching of people or activities.

terrorism—the use of violence or threats of violence to bring about political or economic change.

undercover—disguised in order to gain entry into criminal circles.

white-collar crime—any illegal action in which the criminal deceives victims to gain money or property.

wiretap—a device that cuts in on a telephone wire to enable people to listen to conversations held on the line.

FURTHER READING

Black, J. Anderson. *Organized Crime*. Broomall, PA: Mason Crest, 2003.

De Capua, Sarah. *The FBI*. New York: Children's Press, 2007.

Griffin, Joe, with Don DeNevi. *Mob Nemesis: How the FBI Crippled Organized Crime*. Amherst, NY: Prometheus Books, 2002.

Haugen, David M., ed. *Is the Mafia Still a Force in America?* Farmington Hills, MI: Greenhaven Press, 2006.

Holden, Henry M. *FBI 100 Years: An Unofficial History*. Minneapolis: Zenith Press, 2008.

Kessler, Ronald. *The Bureau: The Secret History of the FBI*. New York: St. Martin's Press, 2003.

Newtown, Michael. *Gangs and Gang Crimes*. New York: Chelsea House, 2008.

Pistone, Joseph D., with Richard Woodley. *Donnie Brasco*. New York: Signet, 1989.

INTERNET RESOURCES

http://www.dc.state.fl.us/pub/gangs/index.html
Maintained by the Florida Department of Corrections, this site provides information about gangs and how they operate.

http://www.fbi.gov/hq/cid/orgcrime/ocshome.htm
The organized crime section of the official FBI Web site has many links to detailed information on important cases and particular kinds of crimes in this area.

http://www.fbi.gov/hq/cid/ngic/violent_gangs.htm
This section of the official FBI Web site focuses on gangs, with links to statistics, discussion of FBI efforts to combat gangs, and stories about some gang cases.

http://www.fbi.gov/fbikids.htm
The kids' page of the official FBI Web site offers activities and information for 6th grade to 12th grade students.

http://www.usdoj.gov/
This is the official Web site of the U.S. Department of Justice.

NOTES

Chapter 1

p. 6: "You push a little . . .": Joseph D. Pistone with Richard Woodley, *Donnie Brasco: My Undercover Life in the Mafia* (New York: Signet, 1989), p. 59.

p. 9: "Penetrating the mob . . .": Louis J. Freeh, *My FBI: Bringing Down the Mafia, Investigating Bill Clinton, and Fighting the War on Terror* (New York: St. Martin's Press, 2005), p. 120.

p. 10: "Before the first trial . . .": Pistone and Woodley, *Donnie Brasco*, p. 11.

Chapter 2

p. 16: "No single individual . . .": quoted in Ronald Kessler, *The Bureau: The Secret History of the FBI* (New York: St. Martin's Press, 2003), p. 113.

p. 19: "If it weren't for the trooper . . .": quoted in Kessler, *The Bureau*, p. 118.

p. 20: "harassment . . . an admission of . . .": quoted in William W. Turner, *Hoover's FBI* (New York: Thunder's Mouth Press, 1993), p. 170.

p. 20: "The core of organized crime . . .": quoted in Michael Woodiwiss, *Gangster Capitalism: The United States and the Global Rise of Organized Crime* (New York: Carroll & Graf, 2005), p. 75.

Chapter 3

p. 25: "Here was a judge . . .": quoted in FBI news story, "A Partnership Is Born: 'Pizza Connection' Only the Beginning," http://www.fbi.gov/page2/may06/falcone051706.htm.

p. 30: "The Teflon Don . . .": quoted in Athan G. Theoharis, ed., *The FBI: A Comprehensive Reference Guide* (New York: Checkmark Books, 2000), p. 306.

p. 31: "They essentially took . . .": quoted in Tom Hays, "Big Mob Case Brings Guilty Pleas, Light Sentences," *Newsweek*, August 14, 2008, http://www.newsweek.com/id/153226/page/2.

Chapter 4

p. 32: "I knew that both . . .": Pistone and Woodley, *Donnie Brasco*, p. 397.

p. 34: "You can't survive . . .": Dick Lehr and Gerard O'Neill, *Black Mass: The True Story of an Unholy Alliance Between the FBI and the Irish Mob* (New York: Harper Perennial, 2001), p. 14.

p. 36: "You can never have . . .": Lehr and O'Neill, *Black Mass*, p. 236.

p. 37: "I thank this court . . .": quoted in City and Region Desk, "$101m Civil Verdict for Wrongful Convictions in Gangland Murder," *Boston Globe*, July 26, 2007, http://www.boston.com/news/globe/city_region/breaking_news/2007/07/judge_to_issue.html.

p. 39: "informing for profit . . .": Woodiwiss, *Gangster Capitalism*, p. 86.

Chapter 5

p. 41: "This is a case of two . . .": quoted in U.S. Department of Justice Press Release, "Two Russian Organized Crime Figures Charged in Plot to Murder Businessmen," March 24, 2006, http://www.usdoj.gov/usao/nye/pr/2006/2006mar24.html.

p. 41: "Most families . . .": Joe Griffin with Don DeNevi, *Mob Nemesis: How the FBI Crippled Organized Crime* (Amherst, N.Y.: Prometheus Books, 2002), p. 17.

p. 43: "My client vehemently . . .": quoted in "The Rudaj Organization aka: The Albanian Mafia," *Johnsville News*, Nov. 2, 2004; updated June 17, 2006, http://johnsville.blogspot.com/2004/11/rudaj organization-aka-albanian-mafia.html.

Chapter 6

p. 51: "almost overnight . . .": quoted in Woodiwiss, *Gangster Capitalism*, p. 111.

p. 52: "a nationwide plague . . .": Robert S. Mueller, III, statement to the House Judiciary Committee, July 26, 2007, http://www.fbi.gov/congress/congress07/mueller072607.htm.

INDEX

Numbers in **bold italics** refer to captions.

About the Author

Dale Anderson lives in eastern Pennsylvania, where he has written dozens of books on history and other subjects. He enjoys cooking, bird watching, movies, puzzles, and sports. He has written three other books in this series.